Taking Leave

Taking Leave

Poems by

Mary Ellen Talley

© 2024 Mary Ellen Talley. All rights reserved.
This material may not be reproduced in any form, published,
reprinted, recorded, performed, broadcast,
rewritten or redistributed without
the explicit permission of Mary Ellen Talley.
All such actions are strictly prohibited by law.

Cover image is a family photo from the author
Cover design by Shay Culligan
Author image by Ken Talley

ISBN: 978-1-63980-470-2

Kelsay Books
502 South 1040 East, A-119
American Fork, Utah 84003
Kelsaybooks.com

Dedicated to my oldest sister Katherine
1938–2023
and her daughter Erin
1964–2018

Acknowledgments

Thank you to the following publications, where versions of these poems previously appeared:

Call of the Morrigan Anthology: "I Inherit Your Name, Morrigan"

Cirque Journal: "Lunar Maria"

Proud to Be, Writing by American Warriors: "Dear Dwight"

Rat's Ass Review: "Attic Noise"

RAISING LILLY LEDBETTER, Women Poets Occupy the Workspace: "Ghazal: Unbuckled Shoes"

Switched-On-Gutenberg: "Phases of the Seven Moons"

Contents

You are from	13
Birdsong	15
Ghazal: Unbuckled Shoes	16
Dear Dwight,	17
Phases of the Seven Moons	19
The Nuisance of Hearing	
(or My Sister Writes Her Own Persona Poem)	20
Attic Noise	21
Interview	22
Villanelle to De-Escalate	25
Arizona Season	26
Erin in Walking Wallenda Mode	27
Texting Cancer	28
Legend of the Fates	30
Messenger Under Arizona Moon	31
Haibun: Having Lit a Votive Candle,	
I Count Butterflies	32
Song in the key of stars	
1. Every star in the universe is singing	33
Song in the key of stars	
2. There is no cosmic erasure	34
One Billion Years Ago Magma Cooled and Here I Stand on	
Enchanted Rock in Texas After I Visit My Sister Whose	
Diagnosis Is Dire	35
We Had Two Different Mothers	36
Orchestral Legacy	37
Glitz	38
I Inherit Your Name, Morrigan	39
Headwaters	40
Lunar Maria	41
She Dreams of Old Faithful	42
My Sister's Landscape of Trains	43

Stairway to Hospice Heaven 44
1956 Playlist 45
Golden Shovel 46
Dear Katherine, 47
Last Palindrome 48

You are from

You are from the same Lilac City Spokane
that I'm from—only you were born in 1938,
with a twelve-year head start on me.

You are from playing in Junior Symphony,
your violin to Fredene's cello and my later violin,
not to mention brother Jim's never-ceasing football.

You are from our Montana farmgirl mom, who
almost drowned at fifteen when North Central teacher,
young Miss Pinkham, said to jump in the deep end.

By the time *old* Miss Pinkham taught your PE class
at North Central High, you said she was as legendary
as the 1908 building's red brick stature.

You are from singing *The Birth of the Blues*
at North Central's annual *Doll Shop* production,
where I swallowed a nickel at intermission.

You are from buying four-year-old me a dress
when Grandpa Pilik took you on the train
to meet his Chicago sisters.

You are from sewing that puffy-pink flower girl dress
I wore for your wedding at St. Francis of Assisi, just
before mom and dad began their eight-year separation.

You are from that *hellish year,* while your husband
flew Medivac helicopters in Vietnam, you parenting
alone in Alabama. Snail-mail letters your only contact.

You are from carrying bits of fabric and paint chips
for home décor, and your purse with damp washcloth
to wipe your children's faces in pre-towelette years.

When I babysat your kids, you insisted on paying me,
although Mom, who rode the bus to teach, said
it was payback for you driving us hither and yon.

When my boyfriend sent roses the summer I visited
you in Alabama, you predicted a future wedding.
You are from being matron of honor in my wedding

and not attending Dad's funeral at St. Francis of Assisi
because your family did an intervention on you.
No liquor since 1987. I raise a glass to you with pride.

You are from mailing fudge to us every Christmas
and from the crèche set we still use
that you gave me and Ken our first married Christmas.

You are from fake fingernails and your own bionic
years: new hip and knee, hearing aids, dentures, pace-
maker, oxygen, and Amulet to prevent a stroke.

You are from smoking for 33 years and now cancer
swinging the grim reaper's scythe. Not your style,
no *sitting on the pity pot*. You are leaving vital signs.

Birdsong

you flit
and whirl
to warm nest
from pine
to chaparral
nest of a cup
holds your mantle
your mate's mantle
new feathers
year after year
all that bright beta-keratin
you fly
to perch in quiet tremulo
grab the first insect
for a snack swallow sip
exhale stale air
from your lungs
preen your feathers
gray and winnowed
by wind
heat dwells
within you
evaporates
to replenish
and shine

Ghazal: Unbuckled Shoes

Her arthritic hip won't bend to reach unbuckled shoes
so she heads to work wearing black unbuckled shoes.

Her husband would grasp her foot to slide it inside
but can't breathe, bend down, reach her unbuckled shoes.

She leaves him with his oxygen hooked up at home—
screen door flapping breezes, like her unbuckled shoes.

Easy on the gas she drives small town streets where trees'
dry limbs reach out to sun like her unbuckled shoes.

Texas dawn, Cracker Barrel Restaurant, she clocks in,
drinks a coffee-cup breakfast in unbuckled shoes.

The custodian props his broom beside her chair,
stops rounds each day to buckle both unbuckled shoes.

They smile as stroller babies throw sandals across
the restaurant floor and parents chase unbuckled shoes.

At 70, she likes spending her store discount,
part-time cashier standing in her now buckled shoes.

This well enough day at its end, she arrives home
with tired feet, now dreaming of unbuckled shoes.

Dear Dwight,

Lucky happenstance for my sister
that your son was at the house
to apply chest compressions
and mouth to mouth.

They wheeled your Vietnam Vet body
into the emergency room
and finally stopped trying.
I wasn't entirely surprised

though I was shocked to read
of your death on Facebook.
I was out of town and no one
had my cell phone number.

Your daughter posted a tribute.
The only signal I caught was her use
of past tense "were" when I paused
in my reading to check messages.

The book said to look at probability
and statistics. This *Whirligig Tour**
relating science warned the laity
to be skeptical of skewed data,

and that there's no such thing
as meaningful coincidence,
mostly vast and random time.
It was 9 am in Spokane.

Nothing remarkable in that.
I had paused to check the internet
at page 121 of my attempt
to counteract my ignorance.

Chemistry:
The author called us
units of carbon
that keep on replicating.

She described *the strongest bond in nature,*
this *covalent bond.* A bit of surprise
when I read of two atoms and teamwork.
Could that refer to you and my sister?

On another page, I read of atoms teaming up
to share charged elements.
Could that mean your three adult children?
I read of electromagnetism

and felt a gut punch current of grief
shudder through me on the sofa.
The book compelled me to find
more coincidences of your gain and loss

and I learned that elements are steadier
and not so volatile
while in a bonded relationship.
Could that have been your long marriage?

I tried to understand the 2nd Law of Thermodynamics,
to know your hundred thousand molecules
remain—though you were ashes
by the time I reached Texas for your funeral.

*Words in italics are from *The Canon, A Whirligig Tour of The Beautiful Basics of Science* by Natalie Angier, Houghton Mifflin Harcourt, 2007

Phases of the Seven Moons

Light most cherished in darkness
waxing crescent
My whole perspective has changed
first quarter moon
She said a whole lotta prayers
waxing gibbous
It gets so lonely evenings
full moon
The short-term memory thing
waning gibbous
These changes so annoying
third quarter
Confront anxiety the beast
waning crescent
This burden shuts the open door
new moon
On the lam body slam
waxing crescent
This burden opens the shut door
first quarter
A casket is the omen
waning gibbous
No matter—ashes scatter
third quarter
Here there everywhere elsewhere
waning crescent
Souls deliver rivers home
full moon
Light white river's edge in sight

The Nuisance of Hearing
(or My Sister Writes Her Own Persona Poem)

It's so fortunate dear Ollie persuaded me
a hearing test might be the better deal
or I'd have waited another year
to start the process. I just gave this spiel

to another friend. Soon all widows in our Fun Bunch
will have hearing aids. No words we kick around
will need repeating. Life's really a fantastic
hearing experience. Now my dishwasher creaks

like a threshing machine and the washing machine's
noisy. I never knew my car's turn signal beeps.
If one aid says low battery I change 'em both,
the wax filters every couple weeks.

Those filters are kind of tricky to remove,
push out the old itty-bitty part being ever so careful
and turn it so I can push out the old and push in
the new. I was feeling a tad irritable

at each inconvenience I do now just so I can hear.
Forevermore! It must sound like I'm pitching a fit.
Wearing these aids is kind of like having kids—
tedious, but on second thought, definitely worth it.

Attic Noise

After I called
to wish you Happy Birthday,
the roof rats threatened
to sneak out
of my attic.

You told me
in your birthday rambling
that our own father
ate a mouse when you were five.
He held a dead mouse,
       his hand   rose,
       his mouth   opened
and you ran
still believing to this day
because you believed then.

Days later now,
my husband carved
a hole in the wall,
trapped two rats
that had traipsed tree to tree
across neighborhoods
and found a weak spot in our roofline.
He was on his way to drop
the bag of rigid rodents in the trash
when I called you in Arizona.

Any scratching
behind the bedroom heat vent
has terminated
but you caution me
that baby rats grow rapidly.

Of this,
you are certain.

Interview

2023

Here I am on an oxygen tether like Dwight was. Eighty-four years old and I finally quit working at the thrift shop. Thought I'd escaped lung cancer. Inoperable. I feel like the rug's been pulled out from under me. I want my ashes at Brad's ranch with Dwight's and Erin's.

2017

It doesn't seem fair that Erin has kidney cancer. Nursing Dwight was expected. This isn't. Her tribe of friends is rallying for her. Like my Grief Group turned Fun Bunch.

2015

Maybe my nose is strong from years of sticking it in other people's business. I told my neighbor no ambulance when I tripped on her tree stump. My nose kept bleeding because of that blood thinner I take. Moran women don't break; we bounce. My sister, Mary Ellen, thinks she's awaiting a rebirth of wonder. But I'm pragmatic. Wait until Fun Bunch sees me for dominos.

2011

Dwight met Mary Ellen's grandson at our grandson's wedding and showed his oxygen tank—told the little guy to call him Uncle Transformer. The V.A. treated him top class. I made apricot bars for his memorial. We'll bury Dwight's ashes at Brad's ranch near Houston. It's not far from Kerrville, where we live now. Dwight liked hunting at the ranch.

1991

My children are grown. Mary Ellen's daughter will be a flower girl for Brad's wedding. Her son will boogie with my eldest, Mike. I'm Katherine now, no more Kathy Jo.

1987

I didn't attend Dad's funeral. I wasn't ready to celebrate my gene pool. My children and Dwight had just done an intervention on me. I got top-notch care at Sierra Tucson. The divorce statistics scared Dwight so he goes to AA meetings.

1973

Living in McMinnville was good. Dwight flew for Evergreen Helicopters. His dad lived with us until the end. Good ol' Pop Palmer. The kids loved camping on the North Fork of the Santiam River. Newlyweds Mary Ellen and Ken would drive down from Seattle.

1970

Calendars keep circling. I was Mary Ellen's matron of honor in March. She and Ken rushed into marriage out of fear over their friends dying in Vietnam. Dwight never told us the gory details of his time there. The Spokane newspaper did print his letter about belly crawling to take Communion at the "altar railing" from the priest prone in the bed of a truck. My Erin was Mary Ellen's flower girl, just as she was mine.

1958

Dwight would drive up in his green '57 Chevy. We'd sit on the front porch of Grandpa Pilik's house where I lived my senior summer. We tied the knot after my sophomore year at WSU and Mary Ellen was my flower girl. Mom finally asked her why she wouldn't talk to Dwight for months. She said he took me away.

1950

I'd walk to my violin lesson on Saturday mornings. Decided I'd name my daughter after Mr. Armstrong's daughter, Erin. Fredene was off with her cello. Jim was on a paper route. Dad was off on his Northern Pacific railroad job. Mom was pregnant with Mary Ellen.

1938

The Catholic Church said save the baby. Mom survived my birth, recuperated. Dad and his teenage sister misread the amount of formula to mix. Mom blamed my later ailments on that early misstep.

1937

If you're going to point a finger, how about blame it on the girdle Mom wore that winter when she was teaching in the one room schoolhouse in Sunnyside, WA. Pregnant and hiding it so she wouldn't lose her job. No married teachers and certainly no pregnant ones allowed. Call it the cramped circle of my early start.

Villanelle to De-Escalate

Twelve years between us, always affection and grace.
Last of our flock of four, I began apart yet not adrift.
Our family taught us what dissonance can erase.

Your plumage and that glamorous smile upon your face,
my 15th birthday at your house gave my ego a lift.
Twelve years between us, always harmony and grace.

We roosted first in Spokane until you flew away,
I eagerly babysat your skittering kids, any day, any shift.
Our habitat taught what too much alcohol can erase.

You and I fledged to our havens slowly, not in any race,
you settled south, me north, we avoided any rift.
Years between us, but I felt your warmth and grace.

House Sparrow and Steller's Jay, we shared, embraced,
celebrated our children, mailed each a birthday gift
though heritage harbored what family tumult can erase.

Stories told as our parents approached death's gates,
until that recent phone call veered us off opinion's cliff.
The years between us, slam damn, there goes the grace.

It's years of goodwill that family chaos can debase.
Will chats between us now seem ill-at-ease, makeshift?
See what scolding twitter or stiff silence can erase.

Today's politics conflate fact and fear with such distaste
that jarring verbal sparring makes talk's axe swift.
Years between our blue and tawny, do we have grace?
Will family ties find harmony that discord can't erase?

Arizona Season

Birds avoid arrows
near perimeters of target practice.
Emily thought hope
the thing with feathers,
touched words within sightline,
put them in her pockets.

Paper wings on a desert willow.
Tufts of concern, given the site,
see the White-crowned Sparrow perched
to ensure her brood is surefooted enough
for insect collection or dung removal.
She lingers until each fledgling finds water

and no errant gale turns into a maelstrom
lest malevolent winds abash safe landing.
Circumstantial evidence
can be a useful predictor
of the small body's ability to endure
despite building a rickety nest

during each rapid infusion of elixir.
Mother says the nest seems overrun
with birds on branches hopping twig to twig.
Without falling, she echoes back
a healing trill, as each fledgling pirouettes
a slow progression toward migratory flight.

Erin in Walking Wallenda Mode

Straight from costume rental, me in a blue gown
with ties hiding my shrinking butt from my besties,

I plant my left foot as the long tube swings
between trees with branches that might save me.

You could call me an elephant as we sway
down the hospital corridor like bricks in a hammock.

If I were a monkey, I'd escape this zoo and use
the tube to jump rope through my pandemonium.

Let me be a Two-tailed Swallowtail butterfly
tricking predators with my streak of blue.

Get a load of this, I'd breathe through spiracles
and suck up nectar with my retractable proboscis!

Walking forward, arms extended like wings,
I sing and dance to earbuds as my slippers slide.

Here comes a clown on stilts to check my vitals
but they must promise not to tell me dire news.

We three will continue to disrupt hospital decorum
while nurses announce the end of visiting hours.

Grandma Moran said, "When you get
to the end of your rope, tie a knot and hang on."

But you know me. I'd jump double Dutch.
They call a group of butterflies a kaleidoscope.

Texting Cancer

Flat pancake on the sofa
Me traipsing to the raised toilet
Absolutely do not want
my mom to wipe my butt
LOL

You know I'd rather
make jokes
TNX to you everyone's
sending cheery cards
YMMD

Dusty apartment
My mom and friends
vacuumed up dog hair

AAMOF
A lotta things
are no longer important
My mom's trying
to get me to eat
My daughter Ash
makes me laugh
when she wants to cry
We're cool

You should see
my skin sag
Mom and I both
wearing long sleeves
to hide our arms
What serendipity
has befallen us
but she's 79 and me 53

OMG
listen to my big words
Stuck here nothing else to do
so I text and text

OTOH
Life is a dilemma
Mom's not Buddhist
but she keeps talking like one
I'd say life's a rollercoaster
and me the lead clown
in this Tucson carny

I digress
BC I miss partying
Gotta go LOL
Morphine calling

IMHO
I wish you didn't choose me
as your dance partner
I'll be AWOL
before you can say
hospice

Key:
LOL Laugh Out Loud, OTOH On the Other Hand
BC Because, YMMD You Made My Day
AAMOF As a Matter of Fact, TNX Thanks
IMHO In My Humble Opinion, OMG Oh My God
AWOL Absent Without Leave

Legend of the Fates

Riddle of the Sphinx.
Doctor says chemo starts this week,
hands us quarters on the dollar
to prolong life. It's pocket change.

Long ago, each Moirai
was attached to fate—
Clotho spun the thread of life,
Lachesis measured, and Atropos cut.

They say a god can save us
from our fate. Call the scalpel, Zeus.
Hera's in the wing. Athena holds
the morphine drip.

Messenger Under Arizona Moon

The black 'n white mongrel, Winston,
didn't bark or budge from his place
on the comforter as I lay next to you

watching your and my painted toes point
at the ceiling sky on a day that turned
out to be just two days before you entered

hospice. We talked of when I babysat younger you,
no mention of cancer cells or prayer. I flew home
before the gauzy moon's final morning

crescent exit. I heard that a black moth
circled your space that day,
and touched each corner of the goodbye room

while your mother moistened your lips.
Your world slowed to a stop
as the sprite flew out your barely open window.

Haibun: Having Lit a Votive Candle, I Count Butterflies

We strategize to keep Painted Ladies in our garden. Offer the protection of leaf clusters. It's ill-advised to pull up thistles. // The doctors congregate to slice and dice. All of that metastasizing did its number. // I want to catch sight of a Blackened Bluewing and a Red-Spotted Purple, those partial to nectar and overripe fruit. A tribe of butterflies is excellent protection. Millions travel south along the Sierra Madre to the Santuario Mariposa Monarca to gather and hibernate on pine and oyamel trees. // Only tripping over the family dog revealed the metastasis. Nothing spells fun like a family trip to the ER. // Aphrodite Fritillary and Dainty Sulphur put on a spectacular show each Spring in the Sonoran Desert.

wings flutter in dense trees
leafy green sanctuary
world of waiting

Song in the key of stars
1. Every star in the universe is singing

I wouldn't go far enough to say   the stars we see
are singing praise   but it is true
that fusion inside stars makes them elongate
resonate just as you   or I would if we oscillated
where we reside   divide   multiply
procrastinate within our resident cavity of mortality
Be careful out there   beware in the slippery space
trying to place every race   until there's no trace

Without someone in the wings   to cling to
you and I remain   empty wallets
valises   suitcases   backpacks   duffel bags
veritable space cadets sans cadences that tether us
weather us   to sound waves' vibratory impulses
We are   one another's Friendship Sevens
for those who   wistfully   listen   glisten
sing to us   cling to us   We are still   in unison

There is a kaleidoscope of women celebrating
a tall goddess   of laughter   who now sparkles
in the sapphire sky   Everyone saying   My oh My
to her fast pitch   no witch   she was one helluva bitch
Her star has not yet been named
Anyone who wants a spit shine   star shine
glass of wine   jug of moonshine   may express
their request   she brighten   their galaxy

See how our closest star dims every bright night
as constellations clamor for attention   One new star
in place   will likely find sidekicks seeking harmony's
déjà vu cacophony   beating off redundancy's
monotony   She'll not   give up laughter   for solace

Song in the key of stars
2. There is no cosmic erasure

All I know is   we remain one another's   sister
brother   Friendship Seven   We bask   surpass
Hubble's reach as nerves wrangle   jangle in the midst
of hope's rope-a-dope that old familiar   slippery slope
Here it comes to be filled anew with James Webb's
infrared insight   dark into light   It's trippy dippy
George Paul John Ringo   You can still   get your kicks
on Route 66   serendipity   Levity is a warm coat
with conch shell in the pocket   We glisten   listen
for harmonics   sing   cling   wing it   in unison

Who knows if we   so inclined   good morning starshine
will be side-by-side   or collide   as we land
Slam the damn contraband   Natural to be
a little bit sad   richly lit   glad   song of the 60s
lyrics to the rooftop   I want to hold your hand
Light travels back   We are galaxies   We have
alacrity   duality   Who said anything about
morality   It's written in the pinhole stars   Count
the light years   Come out   come out wherever you are
Belly up to the bar   with the Tin Woodsman

Oh   oil can of the universe   Be intentional
whimsical   ride a bicycle   with or without
a portable star shield   Don't worry   They'll invent one
by the time we need it   You and I are still
under warranty   We are the Wallendas of wishery
even with our forged certificates of authenticity
needed to legitimately approach a stairway to heaven
Go ask Alice   We undulate a universe of mirrors
The resplendent video drone poohbah   is busy
capturing our endeavors   and collating captions

One Billion Years Ago Magma Cooled and Here I Stand on Enchanted Rock in Texas After I Visit My Sister Whose Diagnosis Is Dire

I salute this monolithic dome,
this vast rising hill of bedrock, roseate granite
that stretches out acres while my sister rests.

I salute my chilled ears and fears buffeted
by a vista of cold wind under afternoon sun,
this dryscape that allows tread of my soles

to tether me to this spread of boulders,
my legs that climb, my knees that check me
from running downhill as I loved to in my youth.

I salute potassium feldspar that makes granite pink,
and gnarly green live oak with roots riveted into rock
atop this sparse terrain where vernal pools of rain

host fairy shrimp, not far from prickly pear cacti,
and blossoms of purple spiderwort.
My own life seems multicolored twists and turns as if

I am the nearby mesquite tree. I would offer my wood
to become hard-sealed flooring in the cowboy art museum
I visit while my sister's body declines. I salute

her oxygen tether and the ibuprofen that I swallow
before each hike. Oh, the raindrops on my face.
They dry before the giant slabs turn slippery.

We Had Two Different Mothers

You say that you've been thinking,
and declare that you and I,
twelve years apart,
(like varied thrush and robin,)
actually had two different mothers.
Yours wore aprons, used Crisco for lotion,
and only wore lipstick for PTA
or Girl Scout meetings—whereas my mom
wore hose and sensible dresses
on weekdays after she went back to teaching
the day I began first grade.
I agree but point out I never knew my mom
to attend school meetings
and at the one Blue Bird meeting I do recall
she fretted when I commented
on the youth of all the other mothers.

Come to think of it, dear sister,
as the last of four,
didn't I also have a different father?
When you were growing up
Dad presided over his horrid castle.
When I turned six, he moved out,
yet kept up appearances at church
so I could be taught by nuns.
Only periodically did his drinking
breathe fire, spew rocks like a dragon.
By the time Mom and Dad
moved back together
they split all costs, groceries,
utilities, and my clothing to the dime.
As child observer, I watched
the coffers of their aging love unlock.

Orchestral Legacy

In the middle
of my sister

our mother placed a wish.

I mean
my sister took that wish
our mother offered
and placed it upon a music stand
in her birth and marriage months.

She turned the pages
of each piece she played
until she spied the double helix,
the one our mother
kept weaving and reweaving,
each woven skein
filled with scales of storied wisdom
composed to rekindle generations.

My sister's music
led her to both diminish

and excel.

Her black case open,
she lifted out her violin
to tuck it snug beneath her chin.

Despite her bold harmonics
and because she had a knack,
the tremor of her vibrato
summoned us to listen
when she played amid the glitter dust
with her well-rosined bow.

Glitz

I ask my sister how long she's featured red
in her living room. She corrects me, *not red but brick;*
you know, I'm very particular about color.

> She bemoans her closets full of fashions, offshoot
> of working resale in retirement, tells me to take
> clothing from her assortment of wild abandon.

A bit crass, but I admit I'm wearing the ring I asked for
when she told me she was dying.
She said to take a bit more from her trove of jewelry.

> How cool it is that DNA gives us both large hands.
> The average woman's ring size is 6 and we are 9.
> Her sterling silver scrollwork fits my index finger.

As I pack to leave from what we both consider
our last visit, and despite our different tastes, I squeeze
three tops and an embroidered jacket into my carry-on,

> wrap my sweater around the rose and gilt ceramic cat
> she sends for my granddaughter's ninth birthday,
> carry it in my large purse I'll hold close on the plane.

Once when I ask the why of jewelry, she says she likes
wearing the flamboyant or the more discreet *depending*
on what mood I'm in. You know, I like looking at them.

> *There may be ego involved. I do enjoy the compliments.*
> She looks at my finger and says I've chosen well.
> Silver ring beside the gold claddagh on my pinkie.

She and I, Celtic contrasts, both of us with hands extended—
counting what fits or doesn't fit—agree we're like our mother.
This hoarding of desire, this preoccupation with *enough*.

I Inherit Your Name, Morrigan

oh, shapeshifter / crow shadow against
full moon / death /oh, slumbering waking /
what is there about distortion / chiaroscuro
smudging / that prepares us to wear
long-forgotten garments / how can / she be both
for death and life / her rough wool / layers
of flowing silk / don't goddesses have to choose /
is she not temptress / of contradictions /
fertility / combines with fog / the crow is hiding
in the dense black / but forgets about silence /
I know the crone is coming back to trick me /
compassion is not her bailiwick / her silence harsh
ink dark / if true her breasts form hills of Kerry /
and she is bird / then mountains fly upon
the breeze / her silver beak / her lips /
my conscience conscientious / disavows her
blame / my sins are plenty / I want her story
to bequeath / healing / for if I spell her name
and drop / r-i-g / from the middle / I see
my maiden name / she is goddess of our family
anger / we are three sisters / cacophony
of outrage at our stumbling / though her sisters'
trinity begot St. Patrick's that we adopted /
I cannot refuse / to juxtapose this goddess
of my contradictions / request that she remain
with me one night / as if upon fog's low layer /
she might wander off / retrieve my mother / father /
sister / brother / through a corridor of messages /
of which the sun is seeking / past or before
laurel / hawthorn / lilac bloom / she retreats
into her shrine / this passage tomb / Newgrange /
where I find / my name / my sisters' names /
upon her lips

Headwaters

Salmon clamor upstream
to lodge their roe
in redd gravel

We are born
on the edge of living
and loss

I don't need you alive
to know
you're my sister

At this point
I'm still using
present tense

You silver-finned
endangered
leap the last habitat

Willows drape
the river edge
with slender sprigs of green

Lunar Maria

The moon is concrete, is a word,
is a divot in the atmosphere,
a splat that changes form
throughout the strife-shelved month.

                It swirls
and I keep confusing rotation with orbit
so much that I am living in sidereal confusion.
Hear me request commutation of synodic interventions.

        No one
but the underserved and undeserved
know what I am attempting to understand.
The planetarium exhibit gives it a simple story.

                      Still, we feel time wax and wane,
spinning disappointment's craters on dry terrain.
Sea of Crises. Sea of Tranquility. Basalt bores hard core
as we forget we're spinning apart.

          The moon will be full
too late for lovers this year   and any who need
an interrupted sky will have to wait one day
to rub a child's back or touch a waning hand.

           The last breath
doesn't seem concrete,
but is, the leaden weight of hearts
hanging by a slender thread.

She Dreams of Old Faithful

The silver ring on her finger
shines in morning sun.
A robin's song chimes from a nearby bush.

She is ready to embrace this grief
of death that spreads layer by layer
on a nest of dry twigs topped by spider silk.

A great nephew's t-shirt says *don't pet the fluffy cows*
as he and his parents mock the fools
who walk close to take photos of Yellowstone bison.

This woman tells her family
she has had her share of life's offering
of *ten thousand joys and sorrows.*

Dreaming, she pitches a tent of grief
and steels herself
for the geyser's hot spray.

My Sister's Landscape of Trains

Does leaving a penny
on the rails
for luck
seem too tame
for a dying act?

What size pebble, stone, boulder
would derail
the whole shebang?
More likely
broken track
or speeding
round a curve
to end of the line,
scattered suitcase,
buried ticket stub.

Stairway to Hospice Heaven

My sister calls to ask if I know the flight arrangements
her son has made, how she tried to call him but his phone
went to message. She needs to know how she'll get to the airport,
and whether to bring more than a carry-on bag.

In a few minutes I realize she's confusing flight time
with when she'll depart this earth—logic blurred by morphine.

I'm overhearing grandkids and my husband in the other room
as they watch Dora the Explorer. I struggle to utter
the "d" word as I ask if she's afraid of dying. The Katherine of old
responds, *Well, of course, I am. Wouldn't you be?*

She goes on to say she believes in a God of love and forgiveness,
but isn't sure if God promises heaven. Long chat—sky darkens—

we hang up. It dawns on me that my force-field sister wonders
whether she'll advance past St. Peter's ledger
to make it inside the pearly gates. I call her back, speak ever so
clearly into her ear: *Katherine, you are going to heaven.*

She needs to know just as sure as Black Eyed Susans
and Purple Coneflowers can grow in her spent Texas soil,

just as sure as she asks her daughter-in-law
to order a new set of fake fingernails—because a dying
fashionista does have standards, you know.
Twenty minutes later she calls again.

I'm tempted to skip the call because I'm settling grandkids—
I answer to hear Katherine thank me for our prior conversation

and speak a quick good night as I stand gobsmacked
by the generosity of the dying.

1956 Playlist

While I was learning to ride
Fredene's old Schwinn, you were
Swinging on a Star with Perry Como.
Dad worked the railroad
but your top pick was Tennessee Ernie Ford
singing *Sixteen Tons* about a coal miner.
You mimicked Doris Day
singing *Que Sera Sera, Whatever Will Be, Will Be,*
and held fake mikes with Fredene
as you two teens harmonized *Sincerely*
with The McGuire Sisters.
In truth, The Platters sang and you told me
you've always been *The Great Pretender*.
It was after WWII—Ike was President
and Patti Page hoped *That Doggy
in the Window* was for sale.
Eddie Fisher crooned *Around the World*.
He hadn't yet ditched Debbie
for Liz and Tony Bennett hadn't left
his heart in San Francisco.
Bing Crosby moved from Spokane
and Grace Kelly became royalty
while they honeymooned
in black-and-white singing *True Love*.

Elvis's hip swivel on *Hound Dog*
and *Heartbreak Hotel* ushered in rock'n'roll.
Little Richard pounded out *Long Tall Sally*
and good-natured Perry Como cheered us
with *Hot Diggity, Dog Ziggity*. Love came true
when Fats Domino found his thrill on *Blueberry Hill*.
How you sang and sang with the Chordettes.
Could their *Mr. Sandman* be your swan song?
You'd prefer that decorum to hearing Bill Haley
and His Comets belt out *See You Later, Alligator.*

Golden Shovel

*after Christopher Howell**

Is the Big Dipper ready for **death?**
"Well, wouldn't you be scared," **says**
the woman who filed a last grievance **this**
coming Monday, in time traveling her **way**
as she carried a brilliant box of silver rings **to**
place on luminescent fingers of stars adrift in **the**
far off Milky Way! She extends each ring to **finish**
promises of shimmery shine to each star next in **line.**

*line from the poem, "Noah at Last"
in Book of Beginnings and Ends

Dear Katherine,

Li-Young Lee wrote,
"There are days we live as though
death were nowhere in the background."

Do you remember the end of summer
when I canned a box of Elbertas
as a birthday gift for Mom?

Her smile was luminous enough
to make her forget her folly
to fall in love with Dad.
Like a jar of peaches,
love may last for years
after the lid pop seal in a boiling water bath,
the rocking roil of canned fruit,
minus stones.

P.S.
I used to call you on
Mom's birthday
just to reminisce.
I can't do that now.

Last Palindrome

Remember me fondly
There are birds outside my window
Song is wafting through trees
Saying goodbye becomes music and breath
Song is wafting through trees
There are birds outside my window
Remember me fondly

About the Author

Born and raised in Spokane, Washington, Mary Ellen Talley migrated to Seattle. She earned a graduate degree from the University of Washington, after which she spent forty rewarding years as a speech-language pathologist (SLP). Poetry has become her second act. She is active in Pacific Northwest poetry circles and contributes book reviews to several journals.

Her poems have received three Pushcart nominations and her first chapbook, *Postcards from the Lilac City,* was published by Finishing Line Press. Her poems have been published in such journals as *Deep Wild, Eco Theo, Ekphrastic Review, Gyroscope,* and *Inflectionist Review,* as well as in anthologies such as *Sing the Salmon Home* and *Raising Lilly Ledbetter.*

Over the years, Mary Ellen has been fortunate to benefit from Pacific Northwest poetry workshops, particularly Poets on the Coast writing retreats with Susan Rich and Kelli Russell Agodon, as well as many classes taught at Seattle's Hugo House. She has learned much from skilled and generous teachers, especially Deborah Woodard, Judith Skillman, Carolyne Wright, Sierra Nelson, John Sibley Williams, Judith Roche, Holly J. Hughes, and Sheila Bender. Sandra Yannone's Cultivating Voices online community has widened her poetry horizons. She is forever grateful to her critique groups, particularly her fifteen years of weekly meetings with the Greenwood Poets, founded by Sharon Cumberland.

Mary Ellen enjoys spending time with her children and grandchildren, bicycling, baking, hiking, and attending live theatre and poetry events with her husband, Ken, her first and trusted reader.

Made in United States
Troutdale, OR
02/05/2024

17465355R00031